# The Big But

## Understanding the Law of Attraction

### by Anita Farrelli

*An ancient Chinese proverb says 'One who asks is a fool for 5 minutes, one who does not ask is a fool forever.'*

This book results from the author herself trying to understand the Law of Attraction for many years. Then one fateful Saturday in June, she sat down to sort her bills on her laptop, and over the space of a day, in a channeled trance, wrote a story about an Archer and his quiver of arrows.

'I sat down at 9:30am and then almost immediately some relatives popped their heads through the patio doors. I jumped up and offered them a coffee as they only drink tea after 12.

They declined the coffee, asking for tea. I had no idea it had gone past 12, as I thought I'd only been sitting at my laptop for just a few moments. I asked them if they were sure it had gone 12 when they laughed and told me it was 4:30pm. I had not moved, had not eaten or drank anything for 7 hours. They asked me what I'd been doing to lose track of time.

Confused, I looked at my laptop and saw the words 'The End.' I told them I appeared to have written a story.'

# Table of Contents

| | |
|---|---|
| CHAPTER 1 | 5 |
| LOTTERY TICKET | 5 |
| CHAPTER 2 | 17 |
| IN PLAIN SIGHT | 17 |
| CHAPTER 3 | 21 |
| JACK | 21 |
| CHAPTER 4 | 33 |
| BIG BUTS | 33 |
| CHAPTER 5 | 42 |
| LUNCH | 42 |
| CHAPTER 6 | 51 |
| YOU USED TO BE GOOD AT THIS | 51 |
| CHAPTER 7 | 60 |
| LOVE | 60 |
| CHAPTER 8 | 69 |
| WORK | 69 |
| CHAPTER 9 | 80 |
| VISUALISING | 80 |
| CHAPTER 10 | 87 |
| CAUSE AND EFFECT | 87 |
| CHAPTER 11 | 94 |
| MONEY, BUTTERFLIES and BATTERIES | 94 |

| | |
|---|---|
| CHAPTER 12 | 108 |
| MONEY | 108 |
| CHAPTER 13 | 114 |
| RETURN | 114 |
| CHAPTER 14 | 118 |
| A NEW DAY | 118 |

# CHAPTER 1
## LOTTERY TICKET

Lydia thought she'd read every book on the law of attraction that she could buy, borrow, or download. She'd watched so many DVD's and videos that she felt she must have a good grip on the subject by now. I mean, she'd been doing this stuff for 10 years, she must be on her way to being an expert, surely?

Although she did sometimes wonder whether if she stopped reading about it and started doing it more by meditating, visualising, and repeating her affirmations, she may see some actual results.

This was a thought process often echoed by her brother, who no longer bought any lottery tickets of his own. He was so convinced she had the handle on this 'manifestation mumbo jumbo' as he called it, that he felt he no longer needed to waste his own money buying them anymore. No pressure there then.

True, there had been some small successes; a holiday to St Lucia (for 2 just as she became single, she ended up taking her brother), a bottle of champagne (still in the wine rack 4 years later) as she had yet to have anything to celebrate) and VIP tickets to the Polo.

She'd had the odd £10 win on the lottery and each time she would say to herself, "Well, if I can win £10, it can't be any harder to win £10 million can it? All I did was buy a ticket?" But the big lottery wins always eluded her. Life was OK, but it certainly wasn't great.

Lydia was standing in the queue at the supermarket, ready to buy her Saturday lottery ticket. She looked at the advert. 'This Saturdays Prize £10 million'

"Hmmm.." she mused to herself "How lovely, what would I do with all that money?"

She decided she would pay off her friends and family's mortgages, buy a boat for her brothers to use, buy a holiday home for everyone, buy a flat for her son (with a cleaner and a cook), buy him a car and put some money aside for her youngest and finally buy her own home again. She'd rented for the last 5 years, since her husband died, and had moved 4 times. Buying her own home would give her the security she desired.

As Lydia was daydreaming she heard the man in front say to the sales assistant, "A winning lottery ticket for tonight please love". The sales assistant laughed and replied, "I'll try my best."

Lydia thought she must hear that a thousand times a day, but then, niggling doubt, crept into her mind. What if that was the actual winning lottery ticket that he bought and Lydia was just wasting her money.

The doubt was always there bubbling under the surface, but she was so desperate for more money. Her car was due its MOT, and she'd been lucky in recent years with small bills, so she was expecting a big hit financially this time.

Just then she heard a voice say,"Yeah, that's right, put your great big BUT in the way again and waste another arrow, haven't you read enough books by now, watched enough DVDs, been to enough meetings to know how this stuff actually works? Stop.Being.So.Desperate!"

"Being desperate means you have all the wrong feelings about wanting money. You're pushing it further away. Just one golden arrow is all I need for my quota. One arrow to hit the target and I can relax for a while, enjoy a few sips of nectar, and have a vacation from your incessant BUT. Trust my luck to be stuck with an OT."

Lydia turned around sharply only to see a man standing behind her texting and yawning. "Sorry," she said to him, "were you talking to me?" The man looked at her vacantly "No, not me love," he replied, shaking his head, and continuing with his texting.

She shook her head and turned back to the sales assistant but then heard, "Holy crapola, did she just hear me? She can't hear me, it's impossible... it's against the rules, I mean it's not even meant to be physically possible. I am going to be in so much trouble over this, maybe she didn't hear me... perhaps it's a coincidence, yeah, that's it, it's just a coincidence, she can't hear me."

Lydia winced, looking from left to right, checking her mobile in case her sons had changed the ringtone again, bought her ticket and left the shop quickly.

"Holy crapola," she said to herself, and chuckled at the thought of being haunted by a 1940s swearing ghost. "Hey, there were some good, kind moments in the 1940s," she heard.

She decided it was probably tiredness and stress as she walked to her car. Things had not been easy recently, and she knew she needed a break both physically, mentally and in life generally.

As Lydia sat in the car sorting her handbag and putting her phone on charge, she mockingly repeated, "Holy crapola"

"Holy crapola, what's wrong with that?"

Without thinking Lydia grinned and replied out loud, "It's so old school, that's what's wrong with it'," chuckling before realising, embarrassingly, that she was alone and talking to herself.

Slumping down into her car seat with a sigh, Lydia opened the chocolate bar she'd bought with her lottery ticket and looked at her reflection in the rear-view mirror. She looked tired and assumed she must be having this conversation in her head, with herself.

She shook her head, took a bite of the chocolate bar, and closed her eyes for a minute.

This had happened once before, when her mother had died. Lydia was convinced that she was having conversations in her head with her dead mother, but her friends and family made her realise it was just wishful thinking.

Her sister had suggested she see a psychiatrist, so Lydia stopped telling people she could still have conversations with her mum. She realised she was probably having conversations with herself anyway but they comforted her and losing her mum so suddenly with 2 small boys to look after on her own, well, she needed a friend. After a few months they stopped and her mind fell silent, well as silent as it can be when you are a single mum to 2 teenage boys.

Lydia sighed, opened her eyes, and screamed in panic. There, looking at her in the mirror, was a face. Someone was sitting in the back seat of her car.

Frantically Lydia opened the driver's door, jumped out and started running away, but then she stopped, realising she needed her car and didn't want the hassle of dealing with the insurance company. All these thoughts ran concurrently through her mind. She found her courage and returned to her beaten up but reliable old car, angry that someone had interrupted her 5 minutes of peace.

Lydia flung open the back door and saw, to her horror, the man was naked and carrying a bow and quiver of arrows. Not registering them as weapons she shouted, "Get out of my car now, you, you pervert."

"Woah, woah, hold on a moment lady, you can see me? Wait, you can't see me, nobody can see me, I'm nonphysical, there's something seriously wrong here."

He looked skyward. "Hilarious, who's messing with me here, jokes over guys, let's just restore the veil" he gestured with his hands "or whatever it is you guys have deleted by mistake, shall we."

Nothing happened. "Oh great," thought Lydia, "Care in the community gone wrong or my sons have stitched me up on one of those TV shows." She looked around nervously, waiting for a camera crew to emerge wishing she'd washed her hair.

Nobody appeared.

They both looked at each other silently for a minute then the naked man with the bow and quiver looked at Lydia, smiled and said "Awkward" and asked, "Why are you calling me a pervert?"

Lydia gasped, amazed that he would ask "Because you are,"... she looked for the right word "a naked Robin Hood... with your squashy bits all over my car seat, that's why, get out of my car!"

"I don't have squashy bits," he objected, as he climbed out of the car to prove it. "They were deemed unnecessary."

"Stay back," she screamed at him. "I know jujitsu."

"Oh, no you don't, you fibber," he laughed.

Lydia fumbled in her handbag for her phone to dial the police, but she realised her phone was still in the car, charging.

She scoured the car park, hoping for another human being to emerge, but the car park was completely empty.

"Are you after my money?" she asked, reaching into her handbag "Here, take my purse."

The naked stranger looked taken aback. "I don't want your money," he said. "In fact, I've been trying to give you more, for like… forever!"

He sat down on the pavement, pouting, and sighed. He tapped the ground next to him.

Although Lydia's heart was still racing from fright, a sense of calm seemed to fall over her. She somehow sensed that he meant her no harm, so she sat down on the pavement next to him.

Lydia placed her hands on her knees and buried her face in them. Muffled, she asked, "Am I going mad?."

"You and me both, kiddo. Sorry I frightened you. Nobody has officially ever seen one of us before," he explained.

"What do you mean nobody has ever seen one of us, what are you? Are you my guardian angel?" she asked and then, before waiting for a reply, "If I can see you, does that mean I am going to die? Oh no, am I having a heart attack, is this an out-of-body experience, are you the, the Grim Reaper?"

The questions tumbled out one after another, ending with "And why the hell are you naked and look oddly like someone I know called Jack?"

"OK, in no specific order, you're both fit and well, the Grim Reaper is not scheduled for another…ah wait, can't tell you that, but nice try, and I can only see one of you so I'm pretty sure you're still in that rather neglected body," he explained as he looked her up and down.

Lydia squirmed, pulling her, ever so slightly too tight, blouse down so that the buttons were no longer straining over her bust. How dare he say neglected.

The naked man continued "I am your Archer, it is my sole purpose to give you whatever you desire, if you allow it, but you have this enormous BUT thing going on which makes my job really, really difficult and all I want is to get one lousy golden arrow on target and then I can have a break. Do you know how long it's been since I had a break from you, 8 years! Why do I look like Jack? I have no idea, but maybe you have a little secret crush on him and want to bump your squashy bits together." he grinned.

Lydia smiled. "I also have a crush on lots of other people. I'd much rather you looked like any of them."

"Close your eyes," he commanded.

Lydia wasn't entirely sure she should close her eyes around a naked man with a bow and arrow, but things couldn't get any weirder, could they?

The Archer spoke, "Now, open them."

Lydia opened one eye and looked to her side. She gasped, looked up and down and up and down again, for there sat next to her, as she giggled, was a naked actor. "Is this better?" he asked in his unmistakable accent. Lydia put her hand out to touch his arm to see if he was real and it felt warm, like human flesh.

She couldn't help but glance down at the groin area and felt her cheeks blush, but there was nothing there. She caught the actor's eye, he grinned, "Now who's the pervert," he said smiling.

Lydia closed her eyes again. "Can we try another one?" she asked. She opened her eyes and another naked actor was sitting next to her. "Hi, is this the form you would like to see?" he asked.

It felt so surreal, as if they were impersonators or wax works come to life. Why would they even be in the same town as her, let alone sit next to her? She realised none of it was real, but she hadn't had so much fun for a long time. She closed her eyes again and relayed a list of men she'd often admired from afar.

Lydia was laughing "Stop please, I can't talk to them. They're all too intimidating," she squealed like a teenager.

The Archer paused, still looking like one of her favourites and with a cheeky wink said, "I know who your secret crush is. Open your eyes now."

Lydia knew the voice, grinned, and slowly opened her eyes to a character from her favourite TV show grinning at her. "Really," he said, "this is your secret crush, you are seriously weird."

"Enough, enough," Lydia laughed. "That was a long time ago. Can we have Jack back please, I definitely do not fancy him anymore and all the others without squashy bits, well that's wrong on so many levels."

She closed her eyes one last time and opened face.

"So, what happens now?" she sighed.

"No idea," he replied.

# CHAPTER 2
## IN PLAIN SIGHT

Large radar screens are positioned all around a massive room with millions of multicoloured blips floating in midair.

Little coloured arrows are flying back and forth. A siren sounds and lights flash, stars and fireworks seem to fill the room. They make an announcement 'Gold on Target' and an Archer walks through the portal door. "7624518 requesting leave Ma'am, Gold on target," they state.

A chair with a sign on the back saying 'The All Knowing' spins around and a shape replies, "Well done 7624518, amazing result as always, permission granted, enjoy"

7624518 exits the room through a door and walks down a pristine white corridor towards a door marked 'Golden Time'. On their way they pass doors marked Babies, Toddlers, School Age, Teenagers, Adults and Retirees.

As they pass the Teenagers door, it opens, and another Archer walks out." My charge just had sex for the first time with their happy ever after, alright!" they say.

7624518 grins, they high five, "See you in Golden Time, my charge just found out she's pregnant, I'm off for some fun times myself."

Just as they lay their hand on the door, they hear an announcement "7624518 back to control please, special request." Turning quizzically they return to control.

As they walk in, the All Knowing's chair spins.

"We have… a situation. A human has seen an Archer."

"That's impossible! No adult has ever seen an Archer, children sometimes as their imaginary friends, but never an adult. Can we not disguise it as a dream or alien abduction story, Ma'am?" They asked.

"Well, we may have done had the idiot not engaged in conversation with their charge and then, for their own amusement, manifested themselves into a variety of actors," they replied.

7624518 offers to replace the rogue Archer.

The All Knowing ponders and then says, "No, let's see how this pans out. Everything happens for a reason and ours is not to question why, but I may need you on hand to sort this mess out if 7624519 fails in their mission."

"Aw, not 7624519, Ma'am," they exclaimed. "They've always been a renegade, doing their own thing, not conforming, not adhering to the rules. Why does it not surprise me they're involved in this."

"We came up through the ranks together. Their record is diabolical, not had a golden arrow on target for 8 years. I'll stand by for the sake of their charge, Ma'am."

"Thank you, 7624518, I've revoked your Golden Time."

# CHAPTER 3
## JACK

On the pavement Lydia appears to the outside world as a crazy woman talking to herself.

Wondering if anyone else can see her naked Archer, she decides it may be better to get back into the car. He follows her and climbs into the back seat.

"Can you please come and sit in the front, you're, creeping me out in the back and can you create, manifest, whatever you do, some clothes please, urgh… do you have a name?" Lydia asked.

"7624519," he answers as he climbs between the seats into the front seat, brushing his naked bottom far too close to Lydia for her liking. "I asked for your name, not your PIN number," she said jokingly.

"We don't have names, just numbers," he explained.

Lydia starts the car and pulls out of the car park, unsure where to go.

"OK," Lydia says, "I'll never remember that, so to make my life easier, I shall call you Jack. Why are you here Jack, what's an Archer and why can I suddenly see and hear you?"

As Lydia drove, Jack explained that the moment a human is born they are allocated an Archer. This has been the way since the beginning of time.

When we're babies, our Archers are babies too and they look like the cherubs depicted in ancient buildings. They grow as we grow. Lydia looked down at her straining blouse and then at Jack's round belly.

Jack grinned "Like looking in a mirror, isn't it?"

Lydia rolled her eyes. She didn't need to be trolled by someone with no genitals she thought to herself.

Jack continued to explain that the Archers role is to carry, 'a never-ending supply of arrows' in their quiver, which are made of bronze, silver or gold, and their mission is to shoot arrows at their charge in response to every 'ask.'

"What do you mean by an ask?" Lydia interrupted.

"I'm glad you 'asked'," Jack replied. "See what I did there?" He giggled to himself and then explained that an 'ask' is something you desire.

Every 'ask' has a level of priority equal to a ratio of happiness.

Bronze makes you feel happy for a short time; silver makes you feel happy for longer, and gold is a life-changing experience.

An Archer will be with you for your entire lifetime. Trying to make your dreams come true and give you all that your heart desires. The only thing that ever stops this is you, and your thoughts.

Jack could see Lydia's confused look. He explained, "Humans create everything in the mental world before it appears in their physical world." He told Lydia that her power to think was unlimited, which meant her power to create, to build any environment she desired, was also unlimited.

Jack paused and looked at Lydia earnestly. "You should be enjoying your life now rather than waiting for it to get better. Have you heard the story of the door in heaven or nirvana, Shangri-La, Utopia or whatever you want to call it?"

Lydia nodded, "Yes, I think so," she replied and repeated the story of the man who passes over and is met by a being that starts showing him around. They kept passing a door and the man asks what's behind the door ,but each time the being says, "Oh nothing, don't worry about that door, it's not important now".

After passing it for the 3rd time, the man stops and demands to look inside the door.

The being stops, unlocks the door, and opens it to reveal a world beyond of such joy and happiness that the man wants to run in and experience it all. "What is this?" he asks. "Who are these wonderful people? That's the girl I always wanted to marry, and that's my dream house. What's going on?"

The being looked at him and told him that this was everything they had wanted to give him when he was human, but he would not allow them to.

"Well remembered, see I told you, you know this stuff," said Jack. "Think of me as kinda the middle being in that story. I have the contents of that room here in my quiver and I can give them to you anytime you want them, but you won't let me. You haven't allowed me to give you anything wonderful for years, sure the odd parking space, bronze arrow, pow! A week long holiday, silver arrow, pow!"

"Are you God?" Lydia interrupted.

"Woah, wait a minute, where did that come from, that's a loaded question."

He explained to Lydia that she had limitless power within her, in her power of thought. She just had to be courageous enough to manifest her heart's desire and then to have the faith to believe it would come to her. That thought needed to be clear and decisive.

Wanting a partner today, thinking maybe not tomorrow, and then thinking OK a few days later would create nothing, as the power of the thought is too scattered. How, can Jack shoot an arrow at a moving target?

Lydia looked confused.

"OK," Jack announced. " Let's simplify this and talk about pies."

"Pies, what like savoury or sweet?" Lydia asked.

"Exactly," Jack replied. " You make pies, I've seen you do it often enough and people seem to enjoy them. When you make the pastry for a sweet pie you add sugar to it and you add salt when you make a savoury pie. If you decide to make a savoury pie and add salt to the pastry but then 5 minutes later you decide to make it a cherry pie you've got the wrong foundations for a cherry pie so you throw that pastry out. "

"Well, actually, I would probably freeze it because, you know…" Lydia interrupted.

"What I'm trying to say is that you have to start from scratch again because you weren't sure what your goal was, whether you wanted to create a cherry pie or a cheese and potato pie when you started creating your pie. If you knew it was a cherry pie the path to pie would have been much easier. All this stopping and starting makes it harder to achieve your goal." He said.

Lydia needed to focus her thoughts, stop changing her mind because of doubt, overthinking things, and then she would get the sweet or savoury success she deserved.

She couldn't be indecisive or negative, couldn't think about disease only health, couldn't think about debt, only wealth, and truth instead of dishonesty. The better thoughts she had, the less bad thoughts she could have. "Plus, your brain only has so much capacity… joking, fill it up with good thoughts of gratitude and happiness, out with the old and in with the new. Keep those vibrations high" He grinned.

"Power of thought?" Lydia queried.

"Oh, so much power," Jack said. He then explained that if he told Lydia there was a spider on the carpet, she would calmly get a glass, a piece of paper, and remove said spider from the premises. He'd seen her do this hundreds of times.

But if he told someone with a fear of spiders that there was one on the carpet their mind would tell them there's danger, they would have a temporary physical reaction, their heart would race, their skin would flush and sweat but the spider is doing the same thing in both scenarios, just simply walking across the carpet.

It's the thoughts creating physical changes in the body, and if thoughts can cause physical changes in the body, then that proves how powerful they can be.

"Anyway," Jack continued, "It's been 8 years since I last fired a golden arrow, when you asked for your job and allowed me to give it to you. You just put up these huge barriers and the biggest is your BUT."

Lydia winced "But I hate my job," she complained.

"Duh… I know, and don't you think I've been trying to change it for you for years," Jack spat back.

He explained, "The job in the school, for example, that was your job, but you had doubts about the journey to work and getting your youngest son to school. The job in the factory, again you thought the start time was too early for you to drive your eldest son to school. The job in the hospital, you blew that one because you worried you wouldn't earn enough." He sighed, "I've got your back kid, always have, always will, but you could have had any of those jobs if you'd just allowed it and focussed on what was best for you at the time too. I could have made things happen to cancel out all those doubts you had."

Jack looked at Lydia and smiled "It's not always about making everyone else happy you know."

Lydia smiled back, she knew that part was true.

Softly he continued, "The only thing that stopped you from having them was your fear, doubt and anxiety, your mouldy old thoughts. Set your intention within, free of fear, doubt and desperation and you can have a wonderful outcome and," he continued, "genuinely believe that you're worthy of what you want."

Lydia was confused; "I really wanted the job in the school. It was perfect. I was really disappointed not to get that one," she whined. "Perhaps I have a duff Archer and you're just a lousy shot," she muttered.

"Oh yeah, that's right, a poor worker always blames their tool." Jack responded. "Perhaps I have a duff human with a massive but."

"Why did you say I was an OT earlier, what does that mean?" Lydia asked.

"Case in point," grinned Jack "It stands for an Over Thinker. Someone who questions and doubts constantly. I mean, there is nothing wrong with that, questioning things, but it makes my job so much harder, not impossible, just harder. It's like you need more discipline over your thoughts, more focus and that's what you need to practice… focusing."

Lydia had decided the safest place to be during her breakdown, or whatever this was, would be at home, so that's where she went. She pulled up on her driveway, glared at Jack, removed her shopping from the boot, and walked to the front door. She paused and turned to see Jack standing right next to her. "Are you coming in?" she asked. It had been a long day already, and she just wanted to get inside and put her feet up.

Jack looked at her quizzically and said, "I'm not a vampire! I don't need to be invited in." He briefly morphed into a TV vampire and pretended to bite her neck. "This lousy house is my home too, you know. I am with you C.O.N.S.T.A.N.T.L.Y have you not got that concept yet?"

Lydia paused as she placed the groceries onto the worktop and suddenly thought about all the times when she would rather have been alone. Eyes wide, she turned and looked at Jack. She blushed. He grinned. "Yeah baby, always, bronze arrow remember, feel good for a short time. Oh, and by the way, I hear your thoughts constantly."

"Ugh… I was right. You are a pervert. I think I preferred it when I couldn't see or hear you. You still haven't explained why I can do both now," Lydia asked as she tried to dodge Jack while putting the groceries away.

"First, I am not a pervert. I am incapable of any sexual feeling. In fact, you make the same face when choosing shampoo as when…"

"OK, OK, got the picture, thanks," Lydia interrupted.

Jack continued. He did not know why Lydia could see and hear him now. To his knowledge this had never happened before, but things were changing, humans were changing, becoming more spiritual and aware and maybe this was some form of an 'intervention', or maybe someone had just pushed a big red button topside by mistake.

Jack's communications had shut down at the same time. He was stranded. He could see other Archers, but they'd been told not to interfere.

Jack and Lydia were in this together whether she liked it or not.

# CHAPTER 4
## BIG BUTS

Lydia was grateful that her sons were staying with their grandparents for a week during holidays. At least the timing was good.  They wouldn't be around to see her meltdown, if that's what it was, and perhaps she could resolve this 'Archer thing' before the boys returned.

They certainly didn't need any fuel for the fire on that count. Her in-laws described her to all and sundry as the 'hippy dippy' type.

Their son had been perfect to them, and she'd never been their choice of daughter-in-law. "I rarely seem to be anyone's," Lydia thought to herself. They were not her choice of in-laws either, but since her husband had died in a car accident 5 years ago, and with her parents dead too, they were the only grandparents her sons had, and she wanted them to have a relationship with them.

They'd had a big row about their eldest grandson just two nights before they collected the boys.

He'd finished his business course and had found himself a job working in a shop to earn some cash, to run his car, and save money to start his own business.

Lydia thought the job sounded awful, tiny salary plus commission on sales and even though she wouldn't have wanted it herself, he was a charming young man, and it may have been a tremendous success for him, so she stayed quiet and praised him.

His grandfather had bought him a car which her son had to pay back monthly , and all was great in the world until her son walked out of the job after 3 weeks saying 'morally' he couldn't do what was being asked of him. He walked straight into a cleaning job so that he could have enough money to pay his grandfather for the car, his car insurance, his mobile phone, but not much else.

Lydia was quietly proud of him for trusting his gut and knowing the job was wrong for him, and having the courage to leave. He wasn't sitting at home watching TV. He'd found an additional cleaning job and was now working 12 hours a day cleaning. She knew it wouldn't last and he would want to find something else, so she was supporting him emotionally and financially through this tough time as best she could, but it was a huge drain on her finances, giving him money for fuel etc.

His grandfather had threatened to take away his car for leaving the job and being irresponsible. The one thing he needed to get back and forward to work to earn money to pay his grandfather back, and pay his insurance. It made no sense to her to take it away from him.

During the argument, Lydia had accused him of being incapable of unconditional love. She'd told him that his love for her husband had come with conditions, get a decent job that he approved of, get a house in the right area, buy the right car and now he was doing it with the boys. Do as I say and I will reward you. Go against me and I will punish you.

He'd pointed his finger at her and spat out, 'You're the problem here. You and your mumbo jumbo the Universe will provide rubbish. You have to work hard for a living.'

Sometimes, with everyone mocking and denigrating her, it seemed like a lonely world and she did sometimes question whether she was indeed the problem.

He could not see that he had the power to create his reality, and that's all their grandson was doing. He'd lined up another job before saying he was leaving and was now working more hours and earning more money than in the original job. It always amazed Lydia how money made some people react.

"No," Lydia had replied, "I think you're the problem, but at the same time you give him contrast and contrast is good because it makes you see what you don't want. Just try to have some faith in him that things will work out OK. He's young, he's entitled to make mistakes and we should support him." she had pleaded.

The sound of her stomach rumbling brought Lydia back to the present, so she set about cooking her dinner. She asked Jack if he'd already eaten. Jack explained he didn't need to eat. She ate her dinner while Jack watched.

He asked her to explain what it all tasted like. She was having cauliflower cheese and tried to explain that cheese tasted creamy, but then he wanted to know what creamy tasted like, but she wasn't in the mood for it, so she settled down on the sofa and turned the TV up.

Jack sat next to her on the sofa and kept asking her to swap channels, something he explained he'd wanted to do for a long time. When an old episode of her favourite TV show appeared, with her secret crush on the screen, they turned and grinned at each other. Lydia laughed and said, "I've seen him naked."

"Yes, but not his squashy bits," Jack replied.

As she was tidying away, Lydia changed channels on the TV to a music channel to play some music. Every time she tried to play a song within a few seconds Jack would shout 'Boring' and she would select another one.

Frustrated, she told him to pick a song. He chose one she hadn't heard since the boys were small. Lydia started dancing, as this was the song she would play to break up arguments with the boys when they were younger. The bongos at the beginning always made them stop and pretend to play the bongos.

"Excellent choice Jack," she shouted over the music.

"This one always raises your vibration, Lydia," he replied as he shimmied and spun across the floor with her.

Exhausted, Lydia took herself off to bed. She looked at Jack and asked him to leave her bedroom but Jack explained that he'd watched over her every night since the moment she was born and he wasn't going to stop now. Despite protesting, he insisted. It felt creepy and yet safe at the same time, but she was so tired.

It had been a weird day and maybe if she slept on it, he'd be gone and perhaps it would all make sense tomorrow.

The next morning Lydia opened her eyes to see Jack about 30 centimetres from her face. "What the... " she shouted. "Morning," he replied "just wanted to see if you could still see and hear me today"

From her reaction it was obvious that she could.

Lydia showered after persuading Jack to stay in the lounge. He was reluctant, as his mission was to be at her side always, but she promised not to have any thoughts while showering and then had breakfast, which was a repeat of last night's dinner.

Jack stopped asking questions when she threatened to have a thought to ask for her Archer to disappear. As Jack wasn't entirely sure if this was possible or not, he decided to play it safe.

As she sat drinking her coffee, Lydia asked Jack more about his opinion of her big butt. She thought this was rather rude, and it wasn't that big anyway.

Jack explained he wasn't talking about her physical butt but her nonphysical BUTS. Lydia was confused.

Jack said that he already knew that Lydia knew about the concept of thoughts becoming real and be careful what you wish for because you might just get it. Well, this is how humans or charges work as creative beings. Every day, whatever age a human is, they're having thoughts, some of which are requests or, as the Archers call them, 'asks'.

Every 'ask' produces an arrow in the Archers quiver. It may be bronze or silver or gold. Jack joked that he thought his quiver had forgotten how to produce golden arrows, as it had been so long. The Archer loads his arrow into his bow and fires it at his charge. Sometimes it hits the target, and the charge receives the bounty, but most times they think 'Yeah but…' and the arrow disappears.

"We call it air bagging," he explained. "We fire at you, you get the doubt, and a big air bag inflates, poof, and we can't deliver it so it pings off or disappears and you are the queen of BUTS!"

"So why are you still with me if I'm so annoying?" Lydia asked.

"Because I can never leave you, you are an amazing creation and I am bound to you for your eternal human life trying to give you everything you desire blah, blah, blah, at least that's what's on the job description." Jack spouted sarcastically.

"Bummer," Lydia grinned, "what's in it for you?"

"If we can deliver complete happiness to you we get to see a little bit of it ourselves in Golden Time, but to do that I have to have a direct hit with a golden arrow and you are the world's best air bagger," Jack sighed.

Lydia had planned to have lunch today with her friend Michelle but she realised this would be impossible with Jack by her side. She picked up the phone to ring her and cancel the lunch date.

"Why are you cancelling your lunch," Jack asked.

"Isn't it obvious?" she replied. "How can I have lunch, in a public place, when you're by my side talking to me incessantly? I'll look like a madwoman."

Jack assured her that lunch was an opportunity and you should never pass by an opportunity. He also assured her he would be as quiet as a mouse.

# CHAPTER 5
## LUNCH

Lydia set off for the restaurant but, as usual, she couldn't find a space anywhere in the restaurant car park. She eventually found a car parking space a short walk away, and set off for her lunch date.

"I could have given you a place in the car park, you know, if you'd allowed me." Jack said "Bronze arrow sat in my quiver."

"So you're the parking fairy too are you," Lydia mocked. "Anyway, it's impossible to find spaces in that car park on a Sunday, especially at lunchtime."

"And so shall it be,.... " Jack muttered to himself.

Just as she turned the corner Lydia saw Michelle pull into a space in the car park, right outside the front door. She thought to herself, "How does she do that, she always turns up late and gets a space closer than anybody. I get here early and have to park miles away… ugh? It's so unfair!"

"That's because she asks for it, believes she's going to get it, because in her experience she always does, and then she receives it, that's all," Jack said.

"I mean come on, you used to talk about the ASK, BELIEVE, RECEIVE mantra with your friend Lyndsey all the time, I like her, she knows about this stuff."

Lyndsey had moved away recently and Lydia missed their conversations. "I must go and visit her soon," she thought.

"I know the books tell you to think about it, but I never really thought of it in such a simple way Jack, " Lydia replied.

Lydia and Michelle settled down at their table for lunch. Lydia had known Michelle for 15 years. They had met on their first day at a new job, but there the similarity ended.

Michelle was a little older than Lydia, a petite size 6, had a loving husband, lived in a beautiful home with no mortgage, took regular family holidays to their villa in Spain and only did charity work now. Her brief foray into the working world had lasted 6 months before interfering with her holiday schedule. Her hair and makeup were always immaculate, and an unknown relative had recently left her a large sum of money. Lydia often wondered why she met up with her, because lunch was always the same.

Lydia would sit and listen to Michelle's woes, rarely sharing her own because the Law of Attraction had told her that if you complain that you have no money you'll create more of the same (lack), but she couldn't sit there and say ' I've just booked a wonderful holiday to Italy for us' or 'I am thinking of changing my car, which of these do you think I should go for?' so she would always just ask Michelle how things were for her.

At the end of lunch, Michelle would always say how much better she felt now that she'd got all that stuff off her chest, and what a good friend Lydia was. Lydia always felt slightly guilty for being a little jealous of her.

Michelle would then take the bill to pay as she knew money was tight for Lydia, and they would arrange to meet up again the following month.

Lydia always left the restaurant feeling a little low, so would call in at her local supermarket and buy a large chocolate bar to cheer herself up. It was a routine she had perfected for the last 5 years since her husband died.

Lydia looked at the menu, deciding what to have. Usually Michelle's lunch would be divine and Lydia's would look as though the cat had thrown it up.

As she was about to order Jack whispered in her ear "How about you ask for your meal to be the best you've ever had here, just for a change, go on, trust me, I could have a bronze arrow here in no time."

"I thought you were going to be as quiet as a mouse?" Lydia muttered quietly.

Jack explained Lydia didn't have to speak out loud as he could hear her thoughts anyway, and he was anatomically incapable of doing what she was suggesting.

"Go on," Jack cajoled. "Ask for your meal to be the best meal you've ever had in this restaurant, I dare you."

Just to shut him up Lydia thought, "I would like this meal to be delicious"… she held the thought for a couple of seconds and then started thinking… "but it hasn't happened yet"

"Stop," Jack's voice made her jump. "Classic air bagging from the human there! Look how big that but was. I had my arrow lined up ready to fire, if you could have just sustained your desire for a few seconds longer I could have hit you with it, but no, not Miss Lydia here with her massive nonphysical but blocking everything coming her way..." he continued on for a few more seconds.

Lydia listened to Michelle telling her how the decorator had done a terrible job on the lounge walls and then tried again."I want this to be the best meal that I have ever had at this restaurant," she repeated it over and over again.

From the corner of her eye she saw Jack grinning and a bronze arrow appeared in his quiver. He loaded his bow and said, "Keep thinking it, you're doing really well" He raised his bow and aimed it at Lydia, she smiled and closed her eyes instinctively and as she did, she thought "but I bet Michelle's will be better though". She braced herself for the impact of the arrow, but nothing happened.

She opened her eyes to find Jack was looking at her with his hands in his pockets. "Did you fire?" she asked him telepathically. "Yeah, I fired, your meal will be good, but hers will be better. I just spoke to her Archer, and she asked for her meal to be exceptionally good as it usually is when she comes here. Life isn't a competition, you know; we can never run out of arrows. Both of you can have exceptional meals, exceptional lives. You just have to allow it. The only difference between you is that she allows it."

"I didn't feel the arrow though Jack, was I meant to?" Lydia asked him telepathically.

"It's not about feeling the arrow, Lydia, " he replied "It's about thinking the thought and feeling the feeling". Jack sighed.

Lydia's lunch arrived, and it was better than she'd eaten in a long time at this restaurant, but Michelle's looked better. Was Jack right, was she truly a creative being, and she had created a good meal but Michelle had just created an even better one. In her head Lydia thought, "I did it Jack, I manifested a good meal"

"And you can do so much more," Jack replied excitedly "don't let things outside of you interrupt your thoughts and don't have these awful mouldy thoughts you seem to love."

Jack started laughing. Lydia asked him telepathically what was so funny.

Jack reminded her that last week she thought she'd seen a van driving down the street with "Brain Management" written on the side and she'd thought how cool was that, when it was just a fancy font for Drain Management. Lydia blushed at her stupidity and grinned discreetly, remembering the moment.

Jack stopped laughing "You were nearly onto it though last week, because you started thinking that maybe your brain needed unclogging, get out your brain rods and clear your negative thoughts. Let's manifest you a Brain Management Van," Jack joked.

When the bill arrived, Lydia went to pick it up, "I'll get this," she offered.

"Don't be silly darling it's on me, I know you can't afford it," said Michelle, taking the bill "These lunches are like my 'therapy sessions' and you're a lot cheaper than my therapist. I always feel so much better after spending a few hours with you, my treat." She pulled a wad of notes from her purse.

Lydia looked at the large wad of money enviously. She was a little relieved, Michelle always chose the most expensive food and wine. She wondered why she was so poor.

"I can help with that. You just need to shut the gate!" Jack replied.

"Shut the gate?" Lydia repeated.

"Yes, to keep those pesky varmint, mouldy thoughts out," Jack said in a cartoon voice.

Trying to have two conversations, one in the physical with her friend and another in her head, was exhausting.

Lydia set off walking to her car and waved to Michelle as she pulled out of the car park. Michelle wound down her window. "I bet you parked miles away, as usual. Would you like a lift to your car, darling?"

"No, no, I'm literally just around the corner," she lied as she watched Michelle drive off in her new sports car. Just then the heavens opened as a torrential rainstorm decided to make Lydia's day even better.

Lydia mused over why her life was so rubbish as she walked along the street.

"Because you think it is, so shall it be," she heard a now familiar voice say.

"Can we change it then?" Lydia asked.

Jack grinned "Finally!"

# CHAPTER 6
## YOU USED TO BE GOOD AT THIS

Back at home, Lydia realised she hadn't bought her usual enormous bar of chocolate after lunch. Oddly, she didn't feel as bad as she usually did. Had she created a better afternoon, with or without the help of her slightly dippy Archer she thought to herself?

"I'm not dippy!" came a voice from behind her.

"I want to know more, Jack". Lydia curled her legs under her on the sofa and nestled her coffee mug between her hands.

"Tell me how I can get all that my heart desires then Jack, " she instructed.

Jack explained that her life had always meant to have been easy, everything was meant to be easy. She was living in a world of illusion that she could change with her thoughts. Some thoughts were her own, some she'd inherited, and some she'd assumed from people around her. Illusions can change with knowledge and knowledge changes your thinking.

It was like a magic trick, when you don't know how it works it amazes and stuns you, but when you know how it works, your thinking changes so the illusion changes. Lydia needed to tell herself it was easy, and then she could change her reality.

"You used to be so good at this, you know," Jack said, surprising her. "Manifesting your reality, I was always in Golden Time."

"What do you mean?" Lydia was confused. "I grew up in a poor family, have been married twice, I'm a widow with 2 teenage sons, have a job I hate and I've been single for 5 years. When was I ever any good at this?"

Jack explained, and it was like a slide show was playing in front of her eyes.

- Age 16 and wanted a good job. She saw Jack shoot an arrow and deliver a job with career prospects.
- Age 17 and wanted to escape the council estate like Cinderella. Jack shot another arrow and delivered a wealthy boyfriend.
- Age 18 wanted a holiday. Jack delivered 2 holidays. One to France and one to Greece.
- Age 19 wanted a car. Jack delivered an MG sports car.
- Age 20 wanted to marry her boyfriend. Jack delivered via a proposal on 21st birthday.

Jack explained that from here on something happened, and she started doubting her thoughts and her instincts.

Lydia laughed and told Jack she could pinpoint the exact moment.

She'd grown up on a council estate because her father had lost his business when she was tiny, and therefore; they lost the family home. Lydia was smart. She'd passed the 11+ entrance exam but her parents couldn't afford for her to go to the Grammar school so she was told to stay at the local comprehensive.

She left school with good grades and got a job in a department store before meeting her fiancé, by chance, one warm summer evening. Her parents had not been very academic themselves, so there'd been no push from them for her to go into further education, and besides, with 3 younger siblings still at home, they expected her to contribute to the household as soon as she left school.

Her fiancé's family were very wealthy and while most were very welcoming, her future mother-in-law was not. The family owned a string of restaurants and after 5 years of dating and 3 weeks after their engagement, Lydia visited one restaurant to see her fiancé after work. She was greeted by her future mother-in-law, who introduced her to a girl called Fiona and her parents. Lydia greeted them warmly only for her mother-in-law to explain that Fiona was Tim's ex-girlfriend.

Bewildered, Lydia asked Tim later what was happening. Was he regretting their engagement?

Tim was fuming with his mother. Fiona had been a favourite of hers and Tim felt his mother had invited her to give him a chance to reconsider his engagement to Lydia. He had told his mother that he loved Lydia and was going to marry her. Tim told Lydia to ignore his mother's behaviour.

They married, but from that moment on Lydia never really felt worthy in her mother-in-law's eyes. Lydia felt she was second best. She would ask Lydia in front of her friends, over family dinners, where Lydia holidayed as a child, before remembering that Lydia had never been on holiday before she met Tim. It seemed like a constant battle to belittle her. She felt as though she didn't fit into this wealthy world. No longer feeling worthy, Lydia eventually sabotaged it at 26 when she left her husband.

Jack continued with the slide show.

- Age 26 wanted to be an air hostess, delivered an interview with the largest UK airline, which Lydia turned down because other thoughts and fears became her own and she was talked out of it. She settled instead for a safe job in a local bank.
- Age 29 wanted to settle down, delivered a husband and a year later, a baby.
- Age 36 wanted another child, delivered a healthy baby boy.
- Age 42 wanted a new job, delivered current job.

The slides seem to run out from here onward. The odd holiday, raffle win, £10 lottery win, but Jack it seemed, had not had a lot to do for the last 8 years.

Lydia almost felt sorry for him, but more so for herself. Why was she denying herself so much and had she really created all these other things for herself? What was behind her door that she may never see? Jack was posing more questions than answers, it seemed.

He smiled discreetly, Jack wanted Lydia to be so dissatisfied with her life that she craved change.

"Where did I go wrong Jack?" Lydia asked.

"Oh, so many places," Jack chuckled, "But it's not over. In the past, you've let other people's fears become your own, and you've given your power over to other people.

I've been shouting at you "Don't listen to this idiot, they don't have your best interests at heart" but you could never hear me, well actually you could a little, I was the little voice in your head asking you to question it, I tried to give you butterflies in your stomach to make you wonder, but the gap between our worlds was too big for me to give you a slap and say 'Come to your senses woman,' plus it's not really my job to do that. I get told off when I try. You should see my list of reprimands," he laughed.

"You've allowed people to infiltrate your mind with their 'mouldy thoughts' for too long, and the thing about mould is that it spreads further and further when left untreated. Simple thing is, until now, you haven't treated your mould."

Lydia sighed. Pennies were dropping. She twisted to look at Jack, grinned and said, "So really you're an arrow wielding exterminator?"

Concentrate on what you want more of, not what you don't want to grow!" said Jack.

Concentrating was something Lydia was finding it hard to do at the moment as the tiredness overcame her.

"You should only have thoughts that will genuinely enhance your life," Jack continued softly. "Don't think about the past as that's gone and don't think about how the future will pan out. Just stay here and love the present with creative and constructive thoughts. Eventually there won't be any room for mouldy thoughts, because you won't want them."

Lydia agreed it was time for a spring clean of her mind.

"Night Jack," she said as she closed her eyes.

Jack settled down to watch Lydia. He'd been an Archer for so many years and always grew close to his charges even though they never knew Archers existed. He looked at Lydia sleeping, she had known so much sadness, so much loss, so much hardship. He didn't know how long he would remain visible to her but he was going to give her as much insight as he could because, as much as he joked about her being a pain, he couldn't help but be in awe of her bravery.

As he gazed at her adoringly, Lydia rolled over onto her back, and started snoring. Jack rolled his eyes, retrieved some earplugs from his pocket, placed them into his ears and took out a pocket book. He liked to keep a tally of his arrows. He added a number 1 to a column with a picture of a bronze arrow for its title, then scrolled back through the pages, a long way back to see his last entry under a picture of a gold arrow.

Jack looked at the column and said, " Get ready for some action soon buddy, I've got a good feeling about this". The gold arrow curled into a smile.

# CHAPTER 7
## LOVE

The sound of the phone ringing woke Lydia. It was 6:55am, and the alarm was due to go off at 7am.

"Ugghh… whose robbing me of 5 minutes' sleep?" she thought.

"Hi Lids, it's me." It was her younger sister, Catherine.

"You'll never guess who I just got a text from, that guy I met in the bar last week, the one who looked so hot and my friend was all over him. Well, dramatic pause… he just asked me out on a date Friday night to that trendy wine bar in town. Should I go, I mean, he's hot and everything but he could be a player, but he doesn't seem it, he seems like a really nice, cute hot guy so I should go, right? Well, I think I want him in my bed on Friday night… ha thanks Lids, see you soon, brilliant advice as always. Love you lots kiss kiss."

"Love you too Kat," Lydia mumbled to a dead phone.

It seems Seb, the 'really cute hot guy' from last week, is history. Her sister had a new man every week. Lydia wondered how she managed it before thinking to herself "Well, for a start, she doesn't have 2 teenage sons to look after."

She'd had a brief 3 month relationship with a man a couple of years before , and when she broke off the relationship he said, "Not many men will take you on in your situation!" Maybe he was right?

"Oh no, no, no, he was not right, and you have given those words way too much power over the years. Those words are keeping you single today," a ranting voice said, coming from the corner of the room.

"Whatever anyone has said about you in the past is void from now on okay, you decide what you think about yourself. Think about what you have to offer, not what someone else thinks you lack. You're funny, kind, intelligent and some might say, he looked her up and down… sexy, you're a mythical creature, baby."

Lydia was still half asleep. "Oh I'd forgotten about you," she said from under the covers "What are you rambling on about?"

Jack was sitting on the end of the bed wearing a cupid's outfit. He grinned "Today we talk about love and attracting it" He fired a cartoon arrow.

"Well, that's always been a hugely successful part of my life so let's see you give that your best shot, bearing in mind I haven't been in a long term relationship for the last 5 years," Lydia replied sarcastically.

"Ah, you have chosen a 5 year sabbatical because you didn't trust yourself to choose the right person again. You've been selective, that's all, ain't nothing wrong with waiting for the right relationship, rather than jumping into a relationship with anybody, rather than be alone. I keep telling you, it's all controlled by your thoughts. Do you believe your ex was right?" Jack asked.

"Well, I'm still alone, so maybe?" she replied.

"So you think it's impossible to find a man who will fall head over heels in love with you, will think your sons are exceptional, will want to work with you to make you all comfortable and secure and share his life and family with you?" Jack asked.

Lydia thought for a moment "No, not impossible" she said as she wandered to the shower. Jack tried to follow her into the bathroom but she shut the bathroom door behind her. Jack opened it anyway and walked into the bathroom still talking.

"Good, that's a much better thought to have, don't you think?" he shouted over the sound of the shower. "Isn't it possible then that there is the perfect someone for you, that you will just know when you see him and feel that wonderful chemistry? Do you trust me to bring you the right guy?" Jack felt he was on a roll.

Lydia poked her head out from the shower curtain "Did you bring me the last lot, if so, NO!" she shouted back over the sound of the shower.

"Hey, I bought you what you thought you wanted, don't shoot the Archer," Jack shouted back.

Lydia emerged from the bathroom, hair wrapped in a towel, and sighed. "So come on then, Jack, spill the beans. How do I attract the love of my life?"

"I'm already here baby," Jack grinned lounging back on the bed.

"Change your thoughts and hold that thought, that's all you have to do. Instead of saying, It's going to be hard to find a guy to take me and the boys on and I don't own my home or earn much money... blah, blah, blah, say I have been selective over the last 5 years and nobody has made the grade but I now trust that Jack is going to bring me the perfect person. I know they are out there and it won't be long before they come easily into my life and they'll be everything I've ever wanted."

Jack jumped up from the bed quickly, startling Lydia, "Wait a minute, you wrote something to a friend once who asked you why you were still single?" He produced a large screen of Lydia's phone and started scrolling.

"Good grief, is nothing sacred" Lydia scolded as she tried to make the screen disappear by wafting her hands through it.

"Here it is," Jack said triumphantly. She asked why you were still single and you replied, and I quote:

'I know what it feels like to want someone so badly that you can barely breathe. I know what it feels like to kiss someone, and for nothing to exist beyond you anymore, everything dissolves into a bright, white light. I know what it feels like to touch someone so gently, but want to pull them so roughly towards you, so that you merge into one. I know what it feels like to close the door as they leave and have to control the urge to run after them, because you want them back in your arms so badly, because it feels as though your heart has been ripped out. I know what it feels like to see their name on your phone and feel your face lighting up before you open the message. I know what this all feels like and I don't want to settle for anything less.'

Jack fell silent.

"Did I write that?" Lydia asked quietly.

"You did, so you know how to feel in love," he said, fluttering his eyelashes.

Jack continued to explain that Lydia needed to boost the thought with emotion, feeling what it would be like to get a message from her loved one. "Thought and feeling is an irresistible combination. There isn't an arrow on this planet that can avoid that," he told her. "As I keep saying, you are just a big battery."

Lydia looked over at Jack as she got dressed. "You've never said that I am a big battery, what do…" she started, but Jack interrupted her.

He explained she had to practice it regularly until it became automatic. She'd practised thoughts of being alone for so long that she'd forgotten what it felt like to be loved, and that had become her default. She was good at focusing on being alone. Jack explained she needed to feel what it would be like to be loved, practice it, and the more she did, the easier it would become.

Lydia listened. "That does sound nicer," she agreed.

Jack decided to push it a little more. "What happened the other night when you went out with your girlfriends to celebrate Clare's birthday?"

Lydia grimaced.

"All your friends live in the opposite direction to you, and they'd planned lifts together and husbands and partners to collect them. You declined a lift from one friend as you knew it would take them out of their way explaining that you'd ordered a taxi. You all left the restaurant at the same time and you watched as they all left you until finally you were alone, standing on a street, in the rain, waiting for your taxi.

After 15 minutes of a no show you phoned them. They were trying to allocate a driver, they said. After 30 minutes and cat calls from drunks and feeling scared you rang again, and they said it would be 10 minutes.

I watched you fight back tears, frightened, wondering why you are always on your own and then you stopped and said 'Enough, this changes now'. That moment the taxi pulled up and you went home 40 minutes after everyone else. It's time for it all to change you thought to yourself, and it is."

"You're right Jack, it is time to change. I deserve to have someone who cares that I get home safely other than my children," Lydia replied.

Just for a moment a golden arrow flickers in Jack's quiver, too quick for Lydia to see, but she is starting to believe.

In a radar room far away, the 'All Knowing' sees the flicker of a golden arrow on the screen. She looks up "Agreed" is all she says, and she smiles.

Lydia pulls off the driveway and starts her drive to work. She suddenly pulls over to the side of the road and turns to Jack in the passenger seat.

"How is this gonna work?" she asks.

"Trust me," says Jack "It will be fun."

# CHAPTER 8
## WORK

Lydia pulls into the car park, she looks at Jack and grins. "I have no need for your bronze arrows, good sir, I've always been able to get in this car park," she gloats.

"Shoot an arrow 10 minutes before you arrive every day," Jack smirks. Lydia looks at him disbelievingly, not sure whether he's telling the truth. "Really?" she asks. Jack shrugs his shoulders and follows her into work, grinning. There are 170 employees and 220 car park spaces. Considering part-time employees, Lydia is always going to get a space. She was correct; she has no need for his bronze arrows, not yet, anyway.

Lydia signs in and notices her boss is already here. She sighs and realises she's going to have to hit the ground running today. Her boss has been on holiday for 2 weeks and he always goes into meltdown on his first day back. There's nothing outstanding. Lydia has dealt with everything in his absence, but he will scrutinise everything she's done trying to pick fault.

Lydia has been working here for 8 years. She takes her coat off and asks her boss if he had a pleasant holiday.

"Yes, yes," he replied, "but I've had to come back to a heap of emails. I thought you may have monitored them for me and a shed load of work has landed on my desk, too busy to chat. I will catch up with you later. I am closing my door so I can concentrate, don't interrupt me."

"So tell me again why you're still here?" Jack asked.

"I've monitored his emails constantly and there are only 2 which require any action and I've highlighted those in red. There was no work on his desk Friday at 5pm, so I don't know where it came from as we shut the office all weekend?" Lydia ranted.

"Hey calm down," says Jack "I was here remember, I know what you did, but again, why are you still, here?"

Lydia explained it wasn't a terrible job apart from her boss. She had free parking and flexible hours, so if she needed to take the boys to the dentist, she could. She'd been doing the job for 8 years, so it wasn't too difficult. Yes, she needed more hours now the boys were older, but her boss had said there was no budget. Lydia felt trapped in a job she hated. She'd tried to apply for other posts in the organisation, but her boss always blocked her attempts at applying for them.

"What do you really want to do?" asked Jack. "Remember, your mind is the most powerful tool you can use in manifesting your desired reality. Everything you think about is going to reveal itself in your life."

Lydia looked confused.

"What would you love to spend your day doing?" Jack clarified.

"I would love to run my own business, have a gift shop maybe, selling all the things I'd love to buy myself, or a coffee shop serving homemade cakes, be a firefighter. Writing, I love writing, poems, children's stories, stories, yes writing, I love to write, I love words, just words…" Lydia continued and Jack noticed a golden arrow gently appear and recede in his quiver as Lydia's enthusiasm grew.

"What are you going to do with all those words you have on your computer, sitting in those folders in those files, all those words in the notebooks scattered around your home?" Jack enquired.

"Nothing," Lydia laughed. "They're just my random thoughts and notes. Nobody would want to read them."

"But what if they did, and someone thought they were good enough to publish, and you had a book that brought you in enough income for you to earn a living?," Jack prodded.

"People with degrees write books or at least an A level in English, not someone with an O level, not someone like me," Lydia replied.

"Hmm, an interesting thought," said Jack. "Is it your own?"

Lydia was confused again; this was happening a lot this week, so yet again she barked out to Jack, "Explain."

Jack told her that a lot of her thoughts were inherited or assumed, which meant that they weren't her truths. He reminded her in flashback of a conversation with her father when she was a small child.

Her father had recently lost his business, and they were struggling to survive. He was standing in front of Lydia saying, "You can't trust anyone with money, they're selfish con men and only out for themselves." He continued, "People like us are the workers who hold this country up, but we'll probably die within a year of retiring because our bodies will be broken, and the rich ones will sun themselves on their yachts until they're 90."

Lydia's father had died of a heart attack less than a year after retiring. "But that's exactly what happened to my father though," she explained.

"Because that became his reality," Jack interjected. "That and the lack of exercise, 20 cigarettes a day and poor diet."

Lydia had lost her father when her eldest son was 4 weeks old. It was moving to see him.

Jack turned to look at Lydia." Change your thoughts to get the success you deserve" Jack appeared dressed as a fumigator. "We are going to have to fumigate that mind of yours, supercharge it by having a good thought, then attach a wonderful emotion to it."

Lydia tried to swat him away like a fly.

"You only believe what you can see and touch. Just because you can't see a wonderful, loving relationship doesn't mean that it doesn't exist. Millions of people all over the planet are living with them every day. You've just become, temporarily separated from these things."

"Start making mental pictures, get them more and more complete, see the minor detail first and as the detail grows, so will the way it's going to come to you. It's like looking through the lens of a camera and the object is not in focus. By concentrating and focusing, the picture becomes clearer. Everything that has ever been created started as an idea. A gate for example to keep cattle in a field."

"Someone worked out that they could cut a tree down and then they could use the wood to make things. To create a barrier to stop the cattle escaping through gaps in the walls or fences and rather than have a barrier, someone thought of a gate to control the entry and exit. Thought comes before the action, the action creates. Your thoughts are in the notes and they can create a book."

"Were you the Archer for the first person to build a gate?" Lydia asked, grinning. " You seem very invested in this gate business!"

"Maybe I was, very useful thing, a gate," Jack replied.

Seeing he had her attention, Jack continued, "Imagination is the start of every thought. A builder can't build anything until someone has designed the plans. Those plans come from someone's imagination."

"You need to grow your imagination. When you were in the shop on Saturday, you started daydreaming about winning the lottery and then you thought, 'But what if that is the winning lottery ticket and I'm just wasting my money here?'" Jack did a pretty good impression of her.

"Let's go back to the idea that you couldn't get a book published. Do you think it's possible that somewhere in the world there has been a really successful book written by someone without even an O level whose wealthy and not selfish and not a con man?" he asked.

"Of course," Lydia responded immediately.

"So why can't you do it?" Jack asked.

Lydia thought for a moment and then listed a whole number of reasons.

- She'd written a dating advert once and a writer (or so he claimed) told her it was full of split infinitives, which made her sound less intelligent than she was. He offered to rewrite it for her; she accepted, and it sounded like a different person had written it.

- She had sent a poem off to a competition and didn't win.
- She'd entered a children's writing competition and didn't win.

Lydia explained you need connections in the writing world, and she didn't have any.

Jack could see that she was looking for more reasons why she couldn't be a writer.

"What you seem to conveniently forget, is that you had so many compliments on the wittiness of your dating ads. Was there one once when you said 'I can't produce you an heir as I have been neutered, but by way of compensation, I make a good lemon drizzle cake'. Guys thought that was hilarious. You didn't win the poetry competition, but you were highly commended and considering that was your first entry, that's not a terrible result. We Archers can't do our jobs on our own. We need you to believe in you too."

"So, I could write and make a living from it?" Lydia asked.

"Duh, you're already writing. Look at all the stuff on your computer at home, all those notebooks you have scattered around the house.

The easy bit is done and as for connections, just have to trust that if you want them, I can bring them into your life for you. All you have to do is ask."

"Try it now, visualise yourself as a writer." Jack commanded. "Imagine and feel, feel and imagine. What would you see and focus, really focus, when your attention is directed the results are startling? That's when people think you're just lucky. Try it for at least five minutes."

"I've never been any good at creating things by visualising Jack," Lydia protested.

"Well, that's where you're going wrong then," Jack countered and explained that you don't visualise to create something as you create with your thoughts, you visualise to give it energy and to keep the vibration up by pretending something already happened.

He explained "It's also really important to not give it any negativity such as thinking about, a holiday for example, visualising yourself in a fancy bedroom, walking out onto the beach in flip-flops and then thinking 'Yeah, but I'm single and it would be boring on my own', and there you are right on cue, you've allowed negativity to creep in and we know that negativity creates mould and mould grows. The negative has been wiping your good thoughts out, it's like you take one step forward and 2 steps back all the time."

Jack was trying to be supportive, but he had his opportunity to speak and he didn't know how long it would last for. He needed to get Lydia to understand.

# CHAPTER 9
## VISUALISING

"So you think you're rubbish at visualising and yet you can teach others how to do it. What happened last week when you went to visit your friend Laura?" Jack asked.

Lydia thought about it and said they just went for lunch, then back to Laura's for coffee and a quick chat turned into a 4 hour chat fest.

"Yes, but what did you talk about?" Jack prompted.

Lydia laughed as she remembered. Her friend had recently moved to a new house and she'd been single longer than Lydia, but she'd recently found a man who was 'ticking a few of her boxes', shall we say.

"What did you make her do?" Jack asked.

Lydia giggled as she remembered. "We were sitting in her lounge, looking into the garden, and I told her to imagine him standing at the BBQ cooking for all her friends, including me. We joked about him taking his shirt off because he was too hot, and her being concerned that he might splash fat onto himself. I told her to pretend he was coming in for more supplies and she had to, grab his hand as he walked by, to see what he wanted. We pretended he was real, we were both talking to him as if he was there." Lydia smiled at the memory. It was funny.

Lydia turned sharply to Jack. "Oh my goodness Jack, I've just remembered .I spoke to her the following week and 20 minutes after I left she received a message from him and they have been chatting ever since."

"See what I mean," Jack said encouragingly. "You know how to do this. You both talked him into her life and you can talk whatever you want into yours, good or bad, remember?"

He told Lydia to think of her mind as a house, and inside her house she has a library, storing all her memories and thoughts. If Lydia was going to build her house, and her library, Jack argued she'd want the best quality bricks, the best window frames, sturdy doors etc. She wouldn't want crumbly bricks and wonky window frames; she'd want something that she could build and forget about. Otherwise she was going to spend all her spare time maintaining it rather than enjoying it, forever patching this bit, looking at that bit. Doing all this mind maintenance would take away from her time to create.

In stocking her library, she wouldn't want to put books in there with mould as she'd be constantly having to throw them out and keep checking if the mould had infected other books. By only putting good thoughts, or books, into her library, she didn't need to spend any more time maintaining them.

He could see by the constipated look on her face that Lydia needed more clarification.

Jack told her she had to check her thoughts and ask herself if that thought was going to enhance or damage her library. If Lydia thought she looked lovely in a new dress, then that thought required no further maintenance. Done deal, she looked lovely, no further thought on the dress required.

However; if she thought the dress was too short or too tight she was going to be constantly directing her thoughts to that, constantly pulling it down. Then she would be wishing her legs were thinner and the whole time she is wearing the dress she'd be maintaining the thought that her dress was too short and her legs were too fat. Maintaining negative, mouldy thoughts, Jack suggested, and if she was having mouldy thoughts how can she possibly have positive creative ones at the same time?

"Visualise the holiday again, feel the sand under your feet and don't worry about the detail, I've got arrows enough to find you someone to enjoy it with, oh and remember once you've visualised it let it grow, don't keep going back and thinking, 'Well, where is it then?' It's like a seed, it's growing, it's flowering. It knows what to do. Trust me, I've been doing this for a long time."

Lydia tried to visualise the holiday attaching no negative thought to it. She imagined swinging in a hammock between two palm trees with her arm across the chest of her partner as they planted a gentle kiss on her forehead, it felt good.

Jack told Lydia to think of being a writer.

Lydia checked that her boss's door was still closed and shut her eyes again. She felt a little guilty about not doing any work.

She imagined herself in a lovely wood panelled office, sitting in a big leather chair with an enormous desk and a computer in front of her, but it was her office.

On the wall were books written by Lydia Banks, and a gigantic pile of paper was sitting on the desk. An assistant came in and picked up the pile of paper.

She asked "Is this the latest draft to be posted to the publishers Ms Banks" Lydia replied in her head "Yes Sarah, and please call me Lydia". It felt good.

"Good, good," encouraged Jack "Imagine and feel, feel and imagine."

Jack's quiver quivered and a golden arrow appeared.

Lydia opened her eyes. "Ah that felt good Jack but…"

Lydia recognised her but and stopped herself "Jack, that felt good."

By 11am Lydia's boss had emerged from his office. He was a single man with wealthy parents and a wealthy girlfriend. They both worked 4 days a week. Her boss by request and Lydia because despite asking every year, there was no money in the budget to increase her hours.

Lydia had lost track of the number of times her boss had said how he would hate to be Lydia's age and not own his own home outright, how it must make Lydia feel very insecure, and whether Lydia regretted making terrible mistakes when she was younger.

Lydia would smile and think to herself, 'The only terrible mistake I made was taking this job' but in a way her boss was holding up a mirror to what Lydia was unhappy about in her own life, so she should be grateful.

Her boss started telling Lydia all about his wonderful holiday and the fact he may book another as he's just had an endowment mature for £20,000 which he doesn't really need, but it can go into the savings account for a rainy day. Lydia smiled and said, "How wonderful." Inside, Jack knew exactly what she was thinking "I have £23 to last me 5 days. Why is life so unfair?"

Another manager came into the office to see her boss and Lydia got a reprieve.

"We need to talk about money," Jack said.

"Well, I can't lend you any," Lydia smiled "I'm broke."

Lydia asked Jack if they could do it later when they got home, as she really needed to catch up on some work. Jack agreed and was quiet, well, almost as quiet as a mouse, until 5pm.

# CHAPTER 10
## CAUSE AND EFFECT

When Lydia arrived home, she picked up the bills off the mat, and found a microwave meal in the freezer, which she nuked. After dinner, Jack again approached the subject of money. Lydia was reluctant to speak about it.

"Why speak about what I don't have, anyway it's too depressing," she moaned as she closed her eyes and laid her head back on the sofa.

"Okay then we won't just yet, let's talk about cause and effect instead," said Jack. Lydia groaned; this sounded like it was gonna be a lecture.

She opened one eye to see Jack had started a presentation on a screen, in mid air.

"Look, I don't know how much longer you'll be able to see me Lydia, and I need to explain so much, so please listen. I am trying to give you thousands of years of advice in as many hours as you can see me. Some of this won't make sense yet but over time it will, just trust me, and listen," Jack pleaded.

Lydia sat more upright and put on her glasses to indicate she was paying attention. Jack was so invested in schooling her and she realised she needed to be just as invested as his student.

"The sun going down has the effect of the moon rising. Drinking too much water means more visits to the toilet. In the same way, thinking you will always struggle with money has the same effect that you will always struggle with money. The cause is your thoughts about money, and the effect is the lack of it in your bank account because your thoughts are always about the lack of money. Is this making any sense?" Jack asked.

Lydia furrowed her brow and pouted. "Not really, but keep going," she instructed.

"Knowing about cause and effect makes you a better 'bringer of arrows," he explained.

"Bringer of arrows?" Lydia mocked.

Jack ignored her and continued. "A thought is the cause and what happens is the effect or outcome."

"You control your thoughts from within, so if every thought is something you truly desire, then every outcome will be what you truly desire. If you don't like the effect of a thought, change the thought.

Told you this earlier, concentration helps you to control your thoughts and because thoughts are causes, the conditions must be the effects. If we can control the cause, then we can control the effect."

Lydia looked confused.

Undeterred, Jack continued, "If you don't like what you have around you on the outside, change what's on the inside. Change what you have in your mind, and the results will show up on the outside. If you're always thinking about someday having someone to love, then someday is in the future and your love is always gonna be in the future."

"Think about what you're gonna have for dinner with your partner, as if it's already here," he instructed.

"Do you mean 'fake it until you make it' ?" Lydia asked.

Jack ignored her and continued, "Without knowing about cause and effect, your emotions can control you. If your business fails, you might think it's bad luck so you start another, but if you don't address the cause, then the effect is that your business could fail again. The cause could be that you don't truly see yourself as a successful businessperson. You may have little puddles of fleeting success from your magnifying glass, but nothing will change permanently."

"Magnifying glass?" Lydia queried.

"I'll explain that later," Jack said as he continued with the presentation.

"All actions have a corresponding reaction. You jump up, you come back down. Thats the Law of Gravity. Think constructively, every thought you have should benefit every person who will be connected to it. A generous thought is much more powerful than a selfish thought, because more people are going to benefit. It grows bigger and bigger whereas a selfish one will just shrink away. The more you give, the more you get."

"Wait, can we just go back a step" asked Lydia "What do you mean by a thought that has to benefit everyone connected with it? Surely me wanting a boyfriend only benefits me?"

"OK," said Jack. "You have two sons. Don't you want them to have a great relationship with your boyfriend? You have other family members, wouldn't it be nice if he got along with them? He may have children of his own, wouldn't you want all the kids to get along and have a great relationship with you as well as his family? And what about all your friends?"

"Yes, but surely, I can't control any of that?" Lydia replied.

"No, you can't control it, but asking for a wonderfully loving relationship that is to the mutual benefit of all, is in your power."

"Very few people realise that what they see are the effects of their thoughts. Remember when I spoke about a gate to keep the livestock in the field and how it had originated from a thought?"

Lydia nodded.

"Think of, a transatlantic airplane. They're massive and fly from country to country, full of passengers and crew. Before it was a plane, it was pieces of metal and electrics and upholstery all coming from different places to be put together and before that the raw materials had to be sourced. Right back at the beginning, there was a designer who drew the plans, engineers who drew the schematics. The plane was just a thought at this stage, just a thought in someone's head and then it became a drawing on some paper, and then it became real."

Lydia smiled, "Are you suggesting I build myself a boyfriend?" she asked.

Jack rolled his eyes but paused and then said "In a way yes. Think about all the qualities you want him to have. Today's vision can become your dream reality if you believe in the power of you. Humans have known this for a very long time."

Jack quoted, 'Each today, well-lived, makes yesterday a dream of happiness and each tomorrow a vision of hope. Look, therefore, to this one day, for it and it alone is life."

Lydia smiled, "I like that Jack, which film is it from?"

Jack rolled his eyes again, he had his work cut out.
"It's from an ancient Sanskrit poem, but it means today is creating your tomorrow, so make today a good day, full of good thought."

# CHAPTER 11
MONEY, BUTTERFLIES and BATTERIES

Lydia hated talking about money, so dodged the discussion with Jack all evening. She checked the front door was locked, turned off the TV and went upstairs to bed, hoping Jack had forgotten about it.

She had butterflies in her stomach whenever she looked at her bank account recently, the wrong ones, little evil ones with fangs. Every time she passed over her debit card she said a brief prayer "Please don't let it be declined." She loathed the fact she seemed to have zero control over the money in and out of her bank account. She hated the fact that she was continually telling the boys that she couldn't afford to buy them the latest game or take them on holiday or buy her son his first car. Lydia wanted to say "Yes", so much, but the numbers on the bank statement didn't lie and the car he'd seen was £600.

As Lydia's thoughts drifted, she imagined her son's face seeing his own car sitting in the driveway and her handing him the keys. He would be so excited, but when you have £23 in the bank, how can changing your thoughts get your teenage son into his own car?

Jack interrupted, "Allow me to interject here please."

"No Jack, I know you mean well, but there is no way that thinking a happy thought will increase my income," Lydia said as she slid under the duvet.

Jack realised talking about money was gonna be a little harder.

After so many years of surviving on benefits and handouts, Lydia needed to realise that she had the power to change her world for the better, but it had to come from her. The belief had to be hers. She needed to feel worthy of financial success. How was he gonna get her to have a good thought about money and get some pleasant emotion behind it?

"Just because you," he said, pointing both index fingers at her and swirling them in circles, "can't see a million pounds, doesn't mean that it doesn't exist. You know it exists. The bank in town has thousands in the vault. You used to put thousands of pounds into the cash point hoppers ready for the weekend when you worked in the bank."

Lydia remembered sitting in the vault unwrapping the money and loading into the hoppers. She would do it with her friend and they would jokingly put little piles aside for a car, a holiday, new shoes before loading it up.

"There are many contrasts in your physical world, size, shape, colour," Jack continued. "Some you can see and some you can't. In your head you have the same contrasts, knowledge and ignorance. All ignorance is, is a lack of knowledge, but the knowledge always exists, it just hasn't been discovered yet,"

"Please be quiet Jack" Lydia pulled the covers over her head.

Jack realised now was not the right time. He was sculpting a masterpiece here, and a sledgehammer wouldn't work. He just needed to keep on chipping away.

"Your wish is my command," muttered Jack.

"First you're an Archer, then you're the parking fairy, and now you're Aladdin's Genie from the magic lamp? You, my friend, are having an identity crisis," Lydia moaned.

Jack, whilst a little hurt, explained that actually they were the same. In the original Genie in the Lamp story, there were not 3 wishes, there were unlimited wishes, much like Jack's quiver for his arrows. It can never run out.

Lydia slowly emerged from under the covers and listened.

He explained that if Lydia didn't think that changing her thinking process could improve her income, then so shall it be. It won't improve. Did she want that?

"No, obviously not," Lydia said.

Jack continued, "You don't like not having enough money, but if all you are ever focusing on is lack or debt, that's where you are asking me to send all my bronze arrows to create more of the same."

"Wait, a minute," said Lydia "You said your bronze arrows gave a short period of happiness. Thinking about debt doesn't make me happy."

"I beg to differ," replied Jack "You think about having debt and no money so often you must enjoy it, so I just give you what you want. It's your bad habit, only unlike smoking, there's no medication, no 'positive patch' you can slap on your arm and forget about."

"The more you persevere with good thoughts about money, no matter how many times you fail, the next time will be easier. Changing your life for the better means stumbling a few times. When you first learnt to ride a bike you fell off, when you first learnt to drive a car you stalled it." he explained.

"I'm like your subconscious mind; I don't decide if what you're focusing on is good for you or not. That parts not in my job description. I take you at your word, accepting everything you ask for or focus on, which then is reflected in the outside world for you. It becomes a pattern or wave like the sea, once a wave gets momentum it can be hard to stop. That wave can be a fabulous thing for a surfer or a disastrous thing for a fisherman."

"Your desire and your belief have to match. If you have a problem, don't spend any more time focusing on the problem, focus on a solution instead. That's where your attention and energy need to go."

"You can solve every problem you've ever had. Day in and day out, you've found solutions. When you get a cut, your body knows what to do to heal it, it sends millions of intelligent cells to fix it, they just get on with it."

"When you have a problem, your mind is geared up ready to get to work to fix it. Think of your mind sitting in a racing car and you can fuel it with top premium oil or you can fuel it with cooking oil… your choice, but one will work better than the other."

Lydia put her hand up, "Can you put cooking oil into a racing car?" she asked.

"I don't know, maybe, stop interrupting, let's just say you can for the purpose of this example," Jack replied.

"Think of top premium oil as good thoughts and cooking oil being riddled with thoughts of fear and doubt, eventually the cooking oil gives up and you splutter to a halt. That's a mouldy thought not going the distance but if you keep putting more and more cooking oil in you think you are making progress but it's really rubbish, smokey, backfiring progress and you're being lapped continuously by people using top premium oil. You need to change the person at the pump fuelling your car and that person is you."

Jack looked at Lydia, he still had her attention so continued. " As a single parent, you would often not have enough money, sometimes just £2 to last all weekend with 2 young boys who ate like horses, so you came up with the solution of pancakes."

Lydia smiled. Her eldest had told her recently that his friends were so jealous when he said he had pancakes twice a week when they only had them on pancake day. He had only recently realised it was because Lydia had no money for anything else.

Jack continued, "I just give you whatever you are focusing on and you can have endless joy or endless suffering. I cannot emphasise this enough, you really get what you focus on. Concentration helps you to control your thoughts and because thoughts are causes, conditions must be the effects. If you can control the cause, you can control the effect."

"Imagine you have a big magnifying glass. On a sunny day, you can hold a magnifying glass in the sun and create a little puddle of light, which disappears the minute you move the magnifying glass.

"Oh, I love this analogy Jack, I heard it from a friend once and thought it made perfect sense" Lydia interrupted.

"I know believe me, I know, but it's do as I say, not do as I do with you. If you can learn to hold that magnifying glass and focus it in one place long enough, you can create a lasting change. Holding it over a piece of wood on a sunny day for long enough will cause the wood to burn and the effect on the wood is that it's changed forever."

"You are the magnifying glass, and your thoughts are the sunshine. Hold them, focus them and wherever they go, they will leave their mark and change your life forever. Your problem lady is that you overthink everything, and you are just too, slap dash, with your magnifying glass, moving it around willy-nilly. For heaven's sake, just hold it in one place long enough for me to fire an arrow, it's really not that hard."

"How long?" Lydia asked.

"How long is what?" Jack replied.

"How long do I have to hold my focus on a thought, Jack?"

Jack thought about how long it took him to manifest an arrow, load it, and aim it.

"10 seconds should be enough" Jack replied "And don't be anxious about it as that's not a good feeling, it makes me anxious and waver with my arrow, give me 10 seconds or longer and I'll give you something tangible."

"10 seconds of a positive thought will change my life?" Lydia queried

"That and feel the emotion of having it, if you can manage it for longer that would be helpful but feel how great it will be, smile as you think about it."

Jack explained "Emotion is just energy in motion so let's supercharge that sucker."

Jack explained all she had to do was imagine her life as she wanted it to be and feel how wonderful it would feel. Jack reminded Lydia that she had grown up in a really poor environment but she'd married into wealth so her mind had overcome her environment and every other obstacle in her path, but she'd lost her focus when the feelings of unworthiness had crept in. Lydia just needed to be engrossed in her good thoughts so that little else matters.

"Do you remember when I told you, you are all just big batteries?" Jack asked.

Lydia explained Jack had mentioned it, but hadn't expanded on it in any detail.

Jack morphed into a scientist in a white lab coat, and a hologram model of a battery appeared in front of him. He explained that for a battery to work, there must be a complete circuit. The electricity is motion and what it powers depends on what we attach it to. Wind is air in motion, put your washing on the line on a windy day and watch it move. Attach a sail to a boat and you see the boat in motion. Thought is the mind in motion and what it powers depends on what we attach it to, and we attach it to our brain.

Lydia was lost, but let him continue explaining.

"You want a good strong steady wind to move your sailboat, a kite surfer wants a steady wind to sail up into the sky, a gusty wind will make it hard work for both of them, and less enjoyable, so everyone wants the right type of wind. If thoughts are powering your brain, then they should be the right ones, do you agree?" Jack asked.

Lydia nodded in agreement. "Good wind, good thoughts Jack, got it." They both giggled like children as Lydia broke wind and apologised.

Jack continued saying she understood she could create thoughts but she couldn't see the results of them until she saw what had manifested in her environment.

He told Lydia to think of herself as a battery lighting a torch, with her thoughts switching on the battery. The electrons leave the battery and light the bulb. He opened his right hand and it glowed bright. A light bulb appeared in front of Jack with a dim glow. Jack sent the glow from his hand towards the bulb and it got brighter. He then opened his left hand and the brightness flowed so he was holding it in the palm of his left hand. He explained the current has to return to the other side of the battery to complete the circuit. Lydia's thoughts were the current/electrons leaving the battery. The initial glow.

When something is sent out, something must be received back. Whatever she sent out would get back, so sending out good thoughts would make everything shine brighter and then the effect of those brighter thoughts would come back to her brighter. Every time she succeeded, she would get more confidence, have more faith, and gain more power to her battery, and her bulb would glow brighter. She could send out a dull thought and she could still get an effect back, but it would be pretty dull.

"You know the bulb is a metaphor for life, don't you?" Jack enquired.

Lydia nodded.

"Forming a perfect circuit means you're operating in harmony with the Law of Attraction" Jack explained, "Actually, when humans talk about the acronym LOA, you don't realise we Archers call it 'Loading One Arrow', because that's what we do."

"The Law of Attraction is always working. Archers are always in action whether or not you're aware of it, which is why it's so important to make sure the energy you're releasing into the world is the type of energy you're okay receiving back to you. The energy flow never stops. Your heart never stops pumping your blood, does it? The tiniest bit of wind can move a sailing boat, the tiniest thought can start a change, the tiniest charge leaving the battery can light up your bulb.

I told you earlier that I don't think 'Oh that's not a good thing for Lydia, I won't give her that thing she's focusing on', I just do what I do. I give you what I think you want. Whatever you are focussed on. I load one arrow and fire. I mean c'mon" said Jack "People have been explaining this for hundreds of years. As Lydia's default was always humour, she looked at her chest and in response to the battery comment said "I must be a D then" laughing at her own joke.

Jack smiled discreetly, but ignored her before sarcastically explaining that the mechanism is perfect and tremendously powerful, but unfortunately sometimes the operator is inefficient.

Lydia pouted, but thought about how it would feel to have someone hold her hand, interlocking their fingers with hers. The feeling of opening the door to her own home for the first time. The feeling of handing in her notice because her publisher had just sent a big advance cheque. The feeling of knowing that she will always have enough money, love and happiness in her life, if she just allows herself to feel it, and believe it.

Lydia could feel tears running down her face, but she had no idea why. She sat upright, smiled at Jack and said, "You're a fantastic salesperson. OK, let's talk about money."

# CHAPTER 12
## MONEY

Jack felt he was on a roll. He wasn't going to waste his opportunity so he went straight into asking Lydia questions.

"Just say yes or no to these questions I'm going to ask you," he instructed.

Do you want more money?
Do you want your life to change beyond all recognition in a good way?
Would you be excited at the thought of buying your own home?
Do you want to be able to pay all your bills quickly and easily?
Do you want to book a family holiday for all of you?
Fancy seeing yourself happy, content, safe and secure in a loving relationship?

Lydia shouted yes to every single question, then Jack told her to repeat them after him but start them with "I".

Lydia didn't understand what difference that would make, so Jack explained Lydia had to stop thinking of herself as a body or as a mind.

Lydia's eyes widened. 'OK' she thought to herself, 'He's definitely lost it now.'

Jack ignored her and continued to explain that she needed to think of 'I' being in control of her body and her mind, controlling what she does and says, not Lydia.

Lydia imagined a little version of herself, cross-legged, floating above her head. Jack sighed and let it go for the meantime. He reminded her that the words she says out loud influence her world within and her world without.

He told Lydia to say 'I love swimming' out loud; she repeated it.

Jack explained that 'I' had told her she loved swimming. Lydia argued that Jack had told her.

"This may be a bit too advanced for now," Jack said.

Lydia apologised for not taking it seriously and asked him to explain, so he continued, "When you say 'I think' the 'I' tells your mind what you should think, so it has to be constructive. 'I' can be whatever it wants to be. Just repeat these after me and see how different they feel," said Jack.

Lydia repeated:

"I love having more money.

I love how my life has changed in a good way.

I am excited about buying my own home.

I love booking family holidays.

I love seeing myself happy and secure in a loving relationship"

Jack smiled, "And so shall it be."

Worn out, Lydia smiled, took off her glasses and lay her head down onto her pillow. Suddenly it was starting to make sense.

For the first time she realised that she truly did have the power to create her reality, her life. Now that she realised it, she was going to create something wonderful. She had so much that she wanted to ask Jack but a strange tiredness overtook her.

"Is it too late Jack?" she asked, midway through a yawn… "It's never too late Lydia," he replied.

"Why me, Jack?" Lydia asked. "Why was I chosen to see you? There's nothing special about me. Why not some big celebrity or politician?"

Jack replied that success had nothing to do with physical aspects, it was solely to do with the power of your thoughts. There were no favourites. Nobody has more power unless you give it to them.

He explained he'd been an Archer to a person like Lydia in ancient times who was a muse. They were very rare, but inspired others to use their gifts. He could see a lot of those qualities in Lydia. Lydia started miming. Jack laughed, "Not a mime you idiot, a muse" Lydia smiled, she knew what he meant.

Today had been a wonderful day, Lydia thought. She felt so lucky that she'd been chosen to see her Archer and somehow she knew things were going to be going in the right direction from now on, at least that's what she would choose to believe. That she was lucky, deserving, worthy, respected, successful, lovable, and attractive.

It was her racing car, and she was gonna fill it with the best quality fuel. It was her house, in her mind and she was gonna build it with great materials. She'd buy the bigger sized dress.

Lydia decided she was going to enjoy her life now rather than wait for it to get better. She was responsible for her thoughts and, subsequently, her actions. There was no point in waiting for her world without to change when the change had to come from her world within.

She deserved a successful life. If she could imagine sucking a lemon and it physically made her glands in her neck drop, then she could imagine a great life too. She knew she had all the tools in her Brain Management van. Lydia smiled to herself.

"I think everyone should be able to see their Archer. Goodnight Jack, love you, see you in the morning. I have loads more questions and I was wondering if you could explain…Oh, it can wait. I'll talk to you about it tomorrow," she said yawning under the covers.

"Oh no, not yet. I need another day," Jack protested as he felt a familiar tingle and started to fade. "Goodbye Lydia, remember me and…" he managed to say but she was already asleep.

# CHAPTER 13
## RETURN

"Woah, not been here for a while," said Jack as he looked around the familiar sights and sounds in the radar room. "Guess I'm in a whole heap of steaming… for this, but can I just say I didn't knowingly reveal myself; I mean, I didn't even know it was possible…"

The All Knowing spoke "Please shut up 7624519."

Her chair spun around and 7624518 was standing by her side.

"518 long time no see," said Jack sarcastically.

"519 still messing things up I see" said 7624518 to Jack. Then he turned to The All Knowing and said. "Shall I transfer Ma'am to the human called Lydia now?"

"No," she replied abruptly, taking him by surprise.

7624518 backed away.

The All Knowing spoke again "7624519 Whilst…"

"I prefer to be called Jack these days Ma'am if that's OK with you?"Jack interrupted.

The All Knowing spoke again "7624519, while it was initially alarming that the human had noticed you it seems that it was a plan constructed by those higher than me. They 'designed' that you would be seen by someone who could write about you in such a way as to simply explain the purpose of the Law of Attraction."

She continued, "As you know, there are no coincidences. There is only synchronicity. There is no need for you to be seen anymore and you may return to the human form known as Lydia to shoot your golden arrow. Goodbye and good luck Jack."

"But, she still needs to understand more," Jack protested.

"No she doesn't, you were right, she is a muse Jack, a gardener sowing the seed for more discussion. She doesn't need to understand it all. She just needs to start the thinking, the conversations, you did a good job, well done," the All Knowing said as she turned back to the screens.

Jack grinned as he felt himself leaving the room. The All Knowing had called him Jack.

As he faded, he heard 7624518 asking if he could be called Dave. The last thing he heard was The All Knowing saying "Dave, of all the names you want to choose, you choose Dave, mind you that David…."

# CHAPTER 14
## A NEW DAY

Jack watched as Lydia woke from a dreamless sleep. She was feeling refreshed and more positive than she had for a long time. There was a warm feeling in her solar plexus, as though the pilot light had been ignited. She held her hands over her stomach and smiled. Things were good. She felt things were good.

She looked around her bedroom, but there was no sign of Jack. Lydia called his name. Jack moved forward to reply but realised she could no longer see him. Lydia wandered around the house looking for him but he was nowhere to be seen.

"Jack, come back, I need you", she pleaded tearfully. Somewhere in the quiet part of her mind Lydia heard his voice say " No you don't, you've got this. Show me what you can do. Keep my quiver busy babe."

Lydia grinned, it didn't seem to matter that she couldn't see him. She knew he existed. She knew there was 'always' gonna be someone on her side wanting the best for her.

She realised she had to help him though by giving him great things to shoot at. If it wasn't great, why would she want it anyway? She looked in the mirror at her behind. It was definitely smaller; she smiled.

At work Lydia smiled at her boss's comments and imagined her name on the leavers' board. While her boss was at lunch she wrote her name on the board under the leavers section, and smiled to herself. She held the thought for 10 seconds, never wavering, and then 5 more for good luck; feeling how great it would feel handing in her notice.

Jack pulled the golden arrow from his quiver and loaded it up to fire with a smile.

That evening she came home and without eating sat down at her laptop and started typing. She typed for hours about the Archer who showed her a new way of living. She went to work the next day and did the same the next evening. Before long she realised she'd written a book.

When she read it, she laughed out loud. "Crikey, I'm a writer," she grinned.

"Come on then Jack, help me get it out there then," she asked.

When Lydia lost her mother she thought that she would never again have anyone who would have her back like her mum did, but she was wrong.

She now had Jack, and admittedly, he was constantly shooting arrows at her, but they could be good ones as long as she believed herself worthy of them. She had someone in her corner who was always going to be cheering her on. She no longer felt alone, as if she had to do it all by herself.

Before long opportunities started showing up, and Lydia's book landed on the right desk. She was signed up by a publisher and given a large advance. She bought her own home and takes her sons on holiday.

Jack is a regular visitor to Golden Time.

How do I know?

My name is Lydia Banks.

Printed in Great Britain
by Amazon